Good Masters! Sweet Ladies! Voices From a Medieval Village

Laura Amy Schlitz

TEACHER GUIDE

NOTE:

The trade book edition of the novel used to prepare this guide is found in the Novel Units catalog and on the Novel Units website. Using other editions may have varied page references.

Please note: We have assigned Interest Levels based on our knowledge of the themes and ideas of the books included in the Novel Units sets, however, please assess the appropriateness of this novel or trade book for the age level and maturity of your students prior to reading with them. You know your students best!

BN 978-1-60539-060-4

pyright infringement is a violation of Federal Law.

2020 by Novel Units, Inc., St. Louis, MO. All rights reserved. No part of s publication may be reproduced, translated, stored in a retrieval system, or nsmitted in any way or by any means (electronic, mechanical, photocopying, ording, or otherwise) without prior written permission from Novel Units, Inc.

production of any part of this publication for an entire school or for a school tem, by for-profit institutions and tutoring centers, or for commercial sale is ctly prohibited.

vel Units is a registered trademark of Conn Education.

nted in the United States of America.

To order, contact your local school supply store, or:

Toll-Free Fax: 877.716.7272
Phone: 888.650.4224
3901 Union Blvd., Suite 155
St. Louis, MO 63115

sales@novelunits.com

novelunits.com

Table of Contents

Summary	3
Teacher Note	3
About the Author	3
Characters	4
Initiating Activities	5
Performing a Monologue or Dialogue	6
Vocabulary Activities	8
Twenty-one Sections	9

Each section contains: Summary, Vocabulary, Discussion Questions, and Supplementary Activities

Post-reading Discussion Questions	27
Post-reading Extension Activities	29
Assessment	30
Scoring Rubric	36

Skills and Strategies

Thinking
Identifying attributes, compare/contrast, pros/cons, research, evaluation

Vocabulary
Definitions, context, parts of speech, synonyms/antonyms

Listening/Speaking
Oral presentation, listening, performance of monologue/dialogue, discussion, acting

Comprehension
Analysis, main idea, memorization

Writing
Poetry, essay, letter, review, newspaper article, creative writing, descriptive writing, comic strip, eulogy, monologue

Literary Elements
Characterization, setting, theme, figurative language, point of view

Across the Curriculum
History—Middle Ages, culture, religion; Music—instruments, songs; Art—diorama, sketch, painting, drawing

Genre: drama—monologues/dialogues; historical fiction

Setting: English manor, 1255

Point of View: first person

Themes: coming of age, survival, life and death, religion, freedom, social status

Conflict: person vs. person, person vs. society, person vs. self, person vs. nature

Tone: personal, often lyrical, poignant

Date of First Publication: 2007

Summary

A variety of young voices from a medieval manor converge to depict the larger story of life in a different time.

Teacher Note

Because of the historical aspect of this book, religion plays a large role in describing the characters' daily lives. You may choose to notify parents of the book's many references to Catholic tradition and the Catholic Church's historical tension with Judaism. This guide approaches religion from both informative and historical perspectives.

About the Author

Laura Amy Schlitz was born on January 1, 1956, in Baltimore, Maryland. A creative child, she worked onstage at a dinner theater when she was 13 years old. She graduated with a B.A. in Aesthetics from Goucher College in Baltimore in 1977 and became a children's librarian. She also spent a few years touring and writing plays for the Children's Theatre Association of Baltimore. Schlitz's first book, *A Gypsy at Almack's*, was published in 1993 under the pseudonym Chloe Cheshire. The Newbery Medal-winning *Good Masters! Sweet Ladies! Voices from a Medieval Village* was originally written 12 years before it was published for fifth-graders to perform. Other books by Schlitz include *The Hero Schliemann: The Dreamer Who Dug Up Troy* and *A Drowned Maiden's Hair: A Melodrama*.

Schlitz continues to work as a librarian. Her hobbies include making marionettes, playing bridge, quilting, playing the folk harp, and making origami animals.

Characters

Hugo: the nephew of Sir Stephen, the lord of the manor; kills and eats a boar

Taggot: the blacksmith's daughter; does not consider herself beautiful; helps Hugo with his horse and develops a crush on him

Will: a plowboy whose father died; works hard to honor his father and care for his family

Alice: a shepherdess; sings her favorite sheep, Jilly, back to health

Thomas: the doctor's son; training to become a doctor himself

Constance: a disabled girl; is traveling to St. Winifred's well hoping to be healed

Mogg: the daughter of a "villein," or slave; When her abusive father passes away, she helps her family hide their best livestock, a cow, so the lord will not claim it as his own.

Otho: the miller's son; reveals how the miller cheats people; is thus disliked by other children

Jack: Mogg's simpleton brother; secretly befriends Otho even though other children will not

Simon: the son of the wounded knight, Sir Stephen; dreams of becoming a knight himself but, because his family is bereft, he must become a monk to preserve his family's status

Edgar: the falconer's son; releases a sparrowhawk from the lord's mews to save it from Simon's neglect

Isobel: Sir Stephen's daughter; believes her status is ordained by God; Her gown is stained when someone in town throws dung at her.

Barbary: an overburdened girl who throws dung at Isobel and feels guilty

Jacob ben Salomon: a Jewish boy who is friendly to a Christian girl, Petronella, at the stream

Petronella: a Catholic girl who is friendly to a Jewish boy, Jacob, at the stream

Lowdy: the daughter of the man who tends the master's hounds; enjoys animals but hates fleas; mother died when she was young

Pask: an orphan who runs away from his lord in search of a better life in town

Piers: the glassblower's apprentice; could inherit the job if he eventually marries one of the glassblower's daughters

Mariot: the glassblower's eldest daughter; willing to marry Piers

Maud: the glassblower's younger daughter; despises the thought of marrying Piers

Nelly: survived drowning as a newborn; considers herself lucky; helps her family catch eels and frogs; claims to dislike Drogo

Drogo: the tanner's apprentice; enjoys tanning but not the complaints about how tanning pollutes the river

Giles: a beggar; survives by working with his father to deceive the townspeople

Initiating Activities

Use one or more of the following to introduce the novel.

1. Observation: Ask students to examine the map at the beginning of the book. They should become familiar with character names and where they live and try to determine the purpose/role of each "pocket" of people. Ask students to predict where the nobility and peasants live as part of a class discussion.

2. History/Setting: Students should research details about how an English medieval manor in 1255 would have functioned. What type of people lived on a manor? How did the "government" of a manor operate? Students should create illustrated posters titled "Manor-isms" that include interesting facts about medieval culture learned from their research.

3. Brainstorming: Ask students to brainstorm the pros and cons of living in the Middle Ages using the chart on page 31 of this guide. Record their ideas to review after reading the book.

4. Culture: Prior to class discussion, have students explore the basic tenets of The Roman Catholic Church, including the roles of Jesus, Mary, the saints, Heaven, and Hell. These elements will be referenced throughout the text as Catholic traditions that were an integral part of daily life in medieval England. In addition, because many held tightly to the Catholic faith, tensions arose between Catholics and people of other religions. Such tensions are also referenced in the text. In groups of three, students can create illustrated alphabet books based on their research. For each letter of the alphabet, students give a corresponding fact—for example, C could be Crusades, I could be Inquisition, etc.

5. Drama: Review with students how to perform a monologue or dialogue. See "Performing a Monologue or Dialogue" on pages 6–7 of this guide. Assign each student a character in the book. On a predetermined date, have each student perform his or her monologue or dialogue for the class.

Performing a Monologue or Dialogue

The following is a list of guidelines to follow when performing a monologue or dialogue. Performances can also be judged based on these points.

General Guidelines

1. BE THE CHARACTER: There is a difference between presentation and performance. When you present information, you can do so as yourself. When you engage in a performance, you are pretending to be someone or something else. When performing your monologue or dialogue, portray the character you represent as much as possible.

2. REFER TO YOUR SCRIPT: It is acceptable to read your monologue or dialogue. However, your performance should be practiced so that you need only glance at the pages and can spend the majority of your time looking at the audience.

3. MAKE EYE CONTACT: Make eye contact with your audience to establish a connection.

4. MOVE INTENTIONALLY: Limit your movements to those that enhance the point you are making or the story you are telling. Movements should not overpower your words. Avoid unnecessary movements such as swaying or pacing. Some teachers may require you to perform without taking any actual steps. Others may encourage you to move around. Ask your teacher which s/he prefers.

5. ENUNCIATE AND PROJECT: Know what each word in your script means and how to correctly pronounce it. Ultimately, you want readers to hear and understand what you are saying. Practice pronouncing difficult words before you perform. Avoid using filler sounds or words such as "ummm." Speak loudly enough for all of the audience to hear.

6. PRACTICE: Practice for a variety of groups of people before your actual performance. The more helpful feedback you get from others and the more familiar you are with your script and character, the better your performance will be.

Tips

1. SCRIPT: Use a copy of the script on which you can mark. Place it in a hardcover binder, preferably black because black is not a distracting color. Mark the script with a highlighter to help you remember how to say certain words or where to use emphasis. Highlighting will also help you find your place quickly if you forget where you are during the performance. Note: When performing a dialogue, each person should have his or her own copy of the script. The script should contain both performers' parts.

2. ATTIRE: Unless there is a special requirement for the character you are playing, wear solid-colored clothing and simple jewelry when you perform. Ornate clothes and jewelry could detract from your performance or give mixed cues about the character you are portraying. The exception is for characters such as Isobel, who wears a fancy blue dress, and Jacob, who has a yellow patch on his clothing.

3. VISUAL IMPACT: Practice your part while looking at yourself in a mirror. This will help you see how often you can make eye contact with an audience. It might also help you notice unintentional hand movements, swaying, etc., that could detract from your performance.

4. ACCENTS: Should you choose to speak in an accent, make sure your accent is accurate for your character. Additionally, practice so that you continue the accent throughout the performance. Switching in and out of an accent is distracting to an audience. Practice using your accent in front of a friend to make sure your audience will be able to understand you. Remember, it is better to use your own voice than an accent that is inaccurate, inconsistent, or difficult to understand.

5. FEAR OF EYE CONTACT: If making direct eye contact with an audience intimidates you, practice looking directly above the heads of your audience. It may be helpful to identify focal points in the back of the room before you begin performing.

Stage Fright!

If you are scared of performing—even a reading performance—in front of a large group of people, start small. Begin practicing your piece by yourself. Then perform for one or two trusted friends or family members. Gradually perform your piece for larger groups of people. Your teacher may be able to help you form a small group of classmates with whom you can practice.

Vocabulary Activities

1. **Vocabulary Sort and Sentences:** Have students sort the vocabulary words into two groups—"Words I Use Regularly" and "Words I Do Not Use Often or At All." Students must then write a set of ten sentences. Each sentence must use at least one word from each column.

2. **Vocabulary Squares:** Select nine students to sit in three rows of three in the classroom. Give each student a large cut-out of an X and an O. Select two other students to compete. One student is "X," and the other is "O." Student X is asked to define a vocabulary word. S/he must choose one of the nine students sitting in a square to define the word and then state whether s/he agrees or disagrees with the given definition. If Student X correctly agrees or disagrees with the given definition, the sitting student must display the X. If Student X incorrectly agrees or disagrees, the sitting student displays the O. Alternate turns between Students O and X. The first student to have three Xs or Os in a row (vertically, horizontally, or diagonally) is the winner.

3. **Sentence-by-Sentence:** As a class, brainstorm a sentence to start a story. Have students pass around one sheet of paper with the starter sentence at the top. Each student must add one sentence to the story. Each sentence must correctly use one vocabulary word from a posted list. After each class member has contributed to the story, have a volunteer read the story aloud.

4. **Writing:** Have students write a free verse poem of their own using at least five vocabulary words from this guide.

5. **Vocabulary Stump:** Divide the class into groups. Assign each group a set of 30 vocabulary words. The first person in the group will randomly select a word. The rest of the team will collaborate—one person will read out the actual definition of the word while the rest of the team members give false, but plausible, definitions for the word. The first person must then decide which definition is correct. Play proceeds to the right. Players receive one point for each correctly-chosen definition. No points are awarded if the player chooses an incorrect definition. The player with the most points is the winner. If time allows, take the winner from each group and let the winners play a championship round while the rest of the class observes and participates by providing false definitions. The teacher should read all of the contrived and the actual definitions during the championship round.

6. **Part of Speech Race:** Randomly select 20 vocabulary words. Give each student a list of the words, and start a timer. The first student to correctly identify the part of speech for each word as it is used in the book is the winner.

7. **Word Spin:** Assign a different vocabulary word to each student. The student must create a spinner using the vocabulary word. The spinner must be divided into six sections including definition, part of speech, word used in a sentence, illustration, synonym, and antonym. Using a brad, the student must connect a paper arrow to the center of the spinner. Place the vocabulary spinners in a reading center where students can use them.

Hugo: The Lord's Nephew

Hugo, after running from his tutor, discovers boar tracks in the forest. He escapes punishment for leaving his studies when his uncle agrees to let him "hunt like a man" (p. 2) and join the boar hunt. The boar is found and killed, but Hugo continues to see the boar in his dreams.

Vocabulary
scimitars
keening
kindled

Discussion Questions

1. How does Hugo happen upon the boar tracks? *(He leaves his tutor and his studies to wander in the forest.)*

2. Why does Hugo's uncle threaten to flog him "like a boy"? What is his alternative to flogging? What does Hugo think about going into the forest? *(Hugo is in trouble for leaving his tutor. He can escape punishment by joining the hunt for the boar. Hugo seems both excited and frightened to join the hunt.)*

3. Why do you think the text says, "…the man that dies from the wound of a boar/loses his soul, and burns in hell" (p. 3)? Do you think this idea is still commonly accepted? *(Answers will vary. The reference seems to refer to common myths during the Middle Ages.)*

4. Does anything in the monologue evoke action on the part of the performer? *(Answers will vary. Encourage students to note action words or analogies that describe movement. Examples include: "this big" [l. 4, p. 2], "tusks can slice a man, groin to gorge" [l. 21, p. 2], "legs were like straw" [l. 14, p. 3], "Braced myself—end to armpit—shoved" [l. 23, p. 3], and "gasped like a fish" [l. 4, p. 4])*

Supplementary Activities

1. Culture: The Feast of All Souls is known today as "The Day of the Dead" or "El Día de los Muertos" in Spanish. Research places in America where this holiday is celebrated, the cultures that celebrate it, traditions associated with the holiday, and the holiday's significance to its participants. Create an art project related to your research such as an altar, a colorful painting, or a hand-cut tissue paper design.

2. Science: Conduct research about boars. Report what they look like, how and what they hunt and eat, and whether or not you think it is reasonable to consider hunting a boar using only a spear. Create a visual display of your findings.

Taggot: The Blacksmith's Daughter

While the villagers go into the forest to flirt and gather flowers for May Day, Taggot stays behind. She is convinced that she is ugly and will never marry, and she contents herself with her gift of calming horses—that is, until Hugo appears. She assists him with his horse, and he leaves her a sprig of hawthorn—a May Day gift just for her.

Vocabulary
forge
palfrey
wondrous
hawthorn
grievous
anvil

Discussion Questions

1. Hugo overcomes fear to battle a boar, but he still dreams about the scary incident. Taggot feels large and unattractive. How are these two characters the same and different from you and your peers? *(Answers will vary. Universal themes include fear, triumph, the desire to be loved, self-esteem issues, etc. Some students may note the issue of class as being something they can relate to—people with more money or power seeming out of reach to a poorer person. Others may not see this as an issue in their lives. Differences could also include daily aspects of the characters' lives—how they hunt, work for a living, and travel on horses.)*

2. Who do you think Robin is? *(Answers will vary. It seems Robin is Taggot's presumably younger sibling; s/he is referenced as being part of Taggot's family along with her father and mother and would have teased her had s/he seen her blushing in Hugo's presence.)*

3. What does this story show you about the role of women in medieval society? *(A woman who did not fit a traditional ideal of beauty may not have been easily married. Additionally, giving birth posed a great risk—childbirth not only endangered the mother's life but also the child's. In a time when there was little understanding of medical science, children often died at a young age. Taggot's mother tries to reassure her, saying that marriage is not without sorrow. Readers also learn that women were not educated as men were, nor were they expected to learn traditionally "masculine" trades such as that of a blacksmith.)*

Supplementary Activities

1. History: Research the role of a blacksmith in a medieval community. Create a visual display of your findings.

2. Culture: Research May Day as celebrated during the Middle Ages. What is the purpose of the holiday, and how did people celebrate it? Bring visual aids to present your findings to the class.

3. Figurative Language: Taggot compares herself to trembling horses, describing the animals and herself as "big and timid." Select something with which you identify—an animal, object, emotion, etc. Then choose two words that explain how you and your object are similar.

Will: The Plowboy

Will remembers his father's words of wisdom as he dutifully plows the fields. He discusses crop rotation, as well as how his father once stole a hare from the lord so the family could have fresh meat. The background information for this section discusses the three-field system of farming.

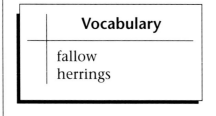

Discussion Questions

1. How is Will's story written differently than Hugo's and Taggot's? Why do you think the author changes style? *(Rather than poetry, Will's story is prose. Consequently, there are complete sentences and paragraphs rather than phrases, lines, and verses. Answers will vary, but the stories were probably written this way for variety in performances.)*

2. Does life seem fair or unfair for Will and his family? Explain your opinion. *(Answers will vary. Will must work the fields though he is young. Some students may think it is unfair to force a child to work instead of going to school. Others may say life is fair for Will's family because they have land of their own and are paid for working the fields. Others may think that the remote location of the family's personal land and the lord's low wages are unfair. Students may comment on the fairness or unfairness of a lord being able to put to death a worker who hunts a hare and eats it—some may think stealing should be punished, while others may believe that Will's family needed the meat.)*

3. What kind of relationship did Will seem to have with his father? How do you know this? *(Answers will vary. They seemed to be close. They worked together even when Will was young. Will's father taught his son about farming and plowing. On his deathbed, Will's father passed along responsibility for the welfare of the family to Will. Will vows to follow his father's direction for the rest of his life.)*

4. Do you think the three-field system made sense for farmers in the Middle Ages? Do you think it was wise for farmers to allow a field to lie fallow every three years? If you disapprove of the three-field system, what other ideas would you propose for growing healthy crops year to year? *(Answers will vary. Encourage students to consider how crops drain fields of nutrients when explaining their positions.)*

5. If you were a young boy in medieval times, would you rather be Hugo (the lord's nephew) or Will (the plowboy)? Explain. *(Answers will vary.)*

Supplementary Activities
1. Science: Research the crops grown in your county or state. What is important in your region for maintaining healthy crops? Write an essay explaining your findings.
2. Culture: Pretend that Will's father was caught stealing the hare from the lord. While the lord has every right to punish Will's father by death, pretend that the lord agrees to hear the plowman's defense. Write a persuasive essay (two or three paragraphs) defending the plowman's decision to steal a hare with the intention of convincing the lord to let him live. Then write another essay on behalf of the lord explaining why Will's father should suffer for his crime.

Alice: The Shepherdess
Alice has a special bond with her sheep, especially Jilly. When Jilly almost dies bearing a lamb, Alice spends the night singing and comforting the animal, hoping to give the sheep the will to live. She succeeds.

Vocabulary
carded
forsake

Discussion Questions
1. Why does Alice's father say Alice is "more sheep than human," and why does Alice claim Jilly is her sister (p. 14)? *(Alice's mother died young, so Alice was raised on sheep's milk. The milk came from the same sheep that bore Jilly.)*

2. What almost causes Jilly to die? *(Jilly gives birth to a lamb that is either dead before it is delivered or that dies during childbirth. With no one to help pull the lamb from the worn-out mother, the mother begins to give up her will to live. Because Alice has fallen asleep, she is unaware of Jilly's distress.)*

3. Consider this quote: "Sheep/don't fight./That's why they need shepherds" (p. 15). How do you perceive a sheep's nature? What role does a shepherd plays in a sheep's life? *(Answers will vary. Sheep are passive and will follow whoever leads them. This makes them easily susceptible to predators. Shepherds must protect their flock.)*

4. Describe the type of conflict in these verses. How is the conflict resolved? *(The conflict is animal vs. nature—Jilly fighting off death. It could also be considered person vs. nature, as Alice helps Jilly overcome death. After Jilly gives up hope of survival, Alice decides to sing to Jilly. Jilly listens to Alice sing all through the night and recovers by the next morning.)*

Supplementary Activities

1. Music: Learn to play the song that Alice sings using an instrument of your choice. Perform the song for the class.

2. Science/Craft: Create a flow chart showing how wool is processed. Include these steps: shearing, washing, dyeing, carding, spinning, and weaving. You can even create an original product from wool yarn to display in class, such as a cap or sweater.

Thomas: The Doctor's Son

Thomas details what he has learned about medicine from his father. He also gives away some tricks the trade doctors employ to protect themselves in the event that patients do not recover.

Vocabulary

comfrey
vanquish

Discussion Questions

1. How is this poem's style different from the previous ones'? *(The earlier stories were told as free verse poetry or prose. This is the first rhyming poem of the book. Each verse follows the pattern aabbccdd.)*

2. Besides knowing about medicine, what other lessons has Thomas learned from his father? *(that you should have patients pay while they are ill, you can scam patients out of food too rich for their diets, and you should overemphasize how ill a patient is in the event s/he dies)*

3. The second footnote names five kinds of fever. Using resources such as the Internet, define each type of fever and deduce how long each type lasts based on the meaning of the fever's name. As a class, discuss whether or not this was a reasonable way to categorize fevers. *(The five fevers are hectic, pestilential, daily or quotidian, tertian, and quartan. Encourage students to look at the root of the words when finding definitions. Hectic fever fluctuates but persists. Pestilential fever likely did not subside and indicated the disease was deadly. Quotidian fever recurs every day. Tertian fever recurs every third day or spikes after every 48-hour interval. Quartan fever recurs or spikes every fourth day or after 72-hour intervals. Answers will vary.)*

4. In what ways are medieval doctors the same and different from doctors today? *(Answers will vary. Suggestions: Doctors then had less research-based information and even referred to the stars to determine a patient's well-being. Their practices were more primitive and experimental than those we use today. However, they also were concerned about liability for patients' deaths, which is the reason doctors today must have malpractice insurance. Doctors then and now both emphasize healthy diets and try to find the best ways to receive payment from patients.)*

Supplementary Activities

1. Science: Research the medieval medical treatments mentioned in the poem, such as bloodletting and using comfrey. Then determine whether or not doctors still use those methods today, and explain why or why not. Write an essay reporting your findings, and remember to cite your sources.

2. History: Research illnesses during the Middle Ages, including battle wounds and plague. What other diseases were common? How long did people usually live during this time? Create a table or chart to enumerate your findings for the class.

Constance: The Pilgrim

Constance, a disabled pilgrim, travels to Saint Winifred's well seeking healing. She recounts the story of Winifred and emphasizes faith in the well's ability to produce miracles. The background section following Constance's story gives general information about why and where people would travel in order to atone for sins or seek miracle cures.

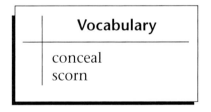

Vocabulary

conceal
scorn

Discussion Questions

1. Why does Constance seek out Saint Winifred's well? Why does she choose the well of this particular saint? *(She wants her crooked back healed and believes that her prayers will be answered if she speaks them at St. Winifred's well. The story of Winifred, according to the poem, tells of a beautiful maiden who survived a beheading when her head was rejoined to her body. Winifred's miraculous healing helps others who are crippled have faith for a miracle of healing as well.)*

2. Discuss the role of saints in medieval times. Why were saints important in this culture? *(Most people in the Middle Ages, particularly in England, were Catholic. Catholic tradition highly esteems saints, and Catholics believe saints have special powers to heal and protect.)*

3. What does this passage tell us about the plight of a medieval person who was disabled in some way? Compare and contrast life for such a person then and now. *(Answers will vary. We learn that Constance conceals herself, may believe her deformity is a sign of God's displeasure, and is sorrowful about her life. Contrasts and comparisons to life for disabled people today will vary, but disability is not generally considered shameful nor a punishment from God, and most disabled people today have access to better health care and can lead independent lives.)*

4. Why do you think people continued to make pilgrimages to holy sites in search of healing? *(Answers will vary. Some people did truly find healing or soothing in special waters or springs. While we can scientifically justify some such cures today, others we still cannot. People continued to have faith because they continued to see results.)*

Supplementary Activities

1. Culture: Research the story of St. Winifred (also known as St. Gwenfrewy). What part of her story is left out of the poem? Where is her well located? Write a short essay filling in information that is left out of Constance's description.

2. Geography/Social Studies: To which locations are pilgrimages popular today and for what reasons? Research one locale and create a brochure promoting the travel/tour trip. Be sure to explain why people would be interested in making the special journey.

Mogg: The Villein's Daughter

Mogg's violent father dies. Because he was a villein, his lord has the right to take the family's best piece of livestock. The family members treasure their cow, Paradise, and hide it when the lord comes, replacing it with a neighbor's lean cow. Consequently, the lord selects a pig and leaves.

Vocabulary
assoil
kingpin
canny
bonny

Discussion Questions

1. What do you know of Mogg's father's character? Is it a blessing or a curse to the family when he dies? *(He was a violent man who hit his family. His wife is blind in one eye, and his son is referred to as a "half-wit" due to the beatings. His death seems both a blessing and a curse because the family can escape his beatings once he is gone, but his death also gives the lord the right to take the best piece of livestock the family has.)*

2. Describe "heriot." Discuss whether or not you think this was a fair practice and why. *(According to heriot, when a villein—a person similar to a slave—died, his lord had the right to take the best piece of livestock he tended. When Mogg's father dies, the lord has the right to take any piece of livestock the family owns. Answers will vary.)*

3. Why does the lord take a pig rather than Paradise from Mogg's family? Explain Mogg's comment, "I'd have chosen the same, in his place" (p. 26). *(Mogg's family temporarily trades their cow for a neighbor's mangy, skinny cow. If Mogg had to choose the best animal, she too would have chosen the pig over the weak, lean cow. She knows the lord is unaware that the family owns Paradise, and they don't retrieve her until the lord has left and it is dark.)*

4. Between Constance, Hugo, and Will, with whom do you think Mogg has the best chance of being friends, and why? *(Answers will vary, but it is most likely Mogg would befriend Will since they are both members of families who work for the lord. Hugo is the lord's nephew and likely associates more with the children of nobility than peasants. Even peasants would probably shun Constance because of her deformity. Most answers will rely on a description of a person's class/economic status.)*

Supplementary Activities

1. Drama: In groups of three, present Mogg's story to the class. Each group needs Mogg, Mogg's mother, and a lord. Using the narration from the poetry, allow Mogg to narrate as the events unfold. The appropriate characters can enact the dialogue.

2. Social Studies: Research laws during the Middle Ages. Create a list of ten that interest you, and provide a brief explanation of each for display in the classroom.

Otho: The Miller's Son

Otho explains the work of milling, including the cheating that happens in order for the miller to have his bread. He feels justified, even though a Judgment Day is coming where he will likely be punished for cheating the people.

Vocabulary
cudgel
sermon
vermin
hypocrites

Discussion Questions

1. Discuss how the author develops the theme of an unchanging cycle in this poem. *(The author uses three methods to communicate this theme—one is the literal meaning of the words themselves. The author repeats, almost like a chorus, "Oh, God makes the water… and the wheel goes/runs on forever" in almost every other verse of the selection. This passage describes God as the source of power for the mill wheel, which will turn forever. The second way an unchanging cycle is described is when the author discusses the "wheel" as "[running] on forever" [p. 29]. This is an image of a circle constantly moving, never changing. The generational story is a third way this theme is discussed. The poem begins with Otho explaining he will be the miller once his father passes on and ends with a reference to Otho treating his future son in the same way his own father treats him now. These generational references show how jobs, temperaments, and even moral compasses were passed from one person to the next during that time.)*

2. Do you agree or disagree with Otho's basic worldview that everyone is a thief, liar, or cheater and that everyone must be a sinner or evil in some way if s/he wants to survive? If you agree, explain why you think his worldview is applicable only in his culture, or if you think it is also true today. *(Answers will vary.)*

3. Why do you think Otho's grandfather was murdered? *(It is likely that the peasants and villeins grew tired of being cheated by the miller and, having no other recourse, decided to kill him. Emphasize to students that violent acts are not acceptable ways to solve problems. In our culture, we have a justice system designed to help people receive fair treatment. Even in the case of Otho's grandfather, the people still suffered at the hands of a cheating miller when Otho's father became the next miller. The murder did not bring justice.)*

4. What do Taggot, Will, Thomas, and Otho all have in common? What does this say about medieval culture? *(They have learned the family trade from their parents and expect to perform the same jobs as the generation before them. Taggot will continue to work as a blacksmith, Will as a plowman, Thomas as a doctor, and Otho as a miller. Answers will vary, though most students should realize that people during this time did not have the same occupational or social opportunities as people have today. Most followed in the footsteps of their parents.)*

Supplementary Activities

1. Culture: Find a recipe for bread that might have been used in medieval times. If possible, use this recipe to bake bread for the class.

2. Science: Build a working model of a grindstone, waterwheel, or bread oven to display in class. Instructions can be found on the Internet. In an oral report, briefly explain how your model works.

Jack: The Half-Wit

Jack describes his life, including being bullied by other children, with the exception of his sister. He secretly befriends Otho, even though Mogg tells him that Otho is a thief.

Vocabulary
jeering
hedge

Discussion Questions

1. How would you describe Jack's character? Do you think he would make a good friend? *(Jack may be a little slow due to his father's beatings [which are referenced in Mogg's story], but he also seems capable and kind. Answers will vary.)*

2. What is Jack's image of Heaven? Why do you think he perceives Heaven in this way? *(For Jack, Heaven is what awaits him after he dies. He envisions Jesus, Jesus' mother, angels, and harmless beasts in Heaven. What he seems to most emphasize is the absence of a presence like his father—one that is abusive or cruel. His conception of Heaven may be based on the Catholic tradition in his culture, but it also seems to be related to his life experiences. Consequently, he longs for a peaceful place where he can associate only with kind family and true friends.)*

3. When Jack finds Otho, what do you think has caused Otho's injuries? *(Answers will vary. From Otho's earlier passage, we know of his father's propensity to beat him. The reader might also assume that other peasants' children beat Otho because he and his father cheat their families out of grain.)*

4. Based on Jack's description of his relationship with Otho, would you consider them friends? Explain. *(Answers will vary. In the classic sense of what it means to be a friend, Jack and Otho are not really friends. However, Jack's definition of a friend is anyone who does not hurt him. Jack therefore considers Otho his friend because Otho treats him kindly by not joining in with the other boys who call Jack names. Other than this, though, Otho does not speak to or smile at Jack.)*

5. What about Jack's story is universal to people in all times and places? *(Answers will vary. The act of bullying, mocking those who are different, name-calling, and even unexpected kind acts such as Jack's could be considered universal elements of the story. Encourage students to use specific evidence from the book and their own experiences or ideas as they answer.)*

Supplementary Activities

1. Writing: Write a story of Jack's encounter with Otho from Otho's point of view. Your story can be written as poetry or prose but must use Otho's voice.

2. Health: Conduct research, and create a brochure a student could use to get help in the event someone is bullying him or her. Some suggested topics are: What is Bullying?; How to Keep From Being Bullied; Ways to Deal With a Bully; Where to Go For Help.

Simon: The Knight's Son

Simon, whose father and grandfather were knights, dreams of one day becoming a knight himself. He is, however, prevented from achieving his dream because the family has no money. To preserve his status, Simon must instead become a monk.

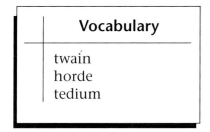

Vocabulary

twain
horde
tedium

Discussion Questions

1. Do you think Simon's vision of a knight's life is realistic? Explain. *(Answers will vary. Simon sees the glory in being a knight. He seems to easily overlook what knighthood cost his family financially and that it took a serious toll on his father's physical well-being.)*

2. How does the author juxtapose Simon's ideals with the reality of battle? *(The author presents Simon's ideals as good and wholesome—for example, his desire to defend widows and orphans, his chivalry, and his pureness of heart. After describing Simon's desire to be a faithful, good-hearted knight, the author depicts the reality of life in battle—slashing, crushing, and killing. Such violence is opposite to the ideals presented in the previous lines of the verse. However, both the dream and the reality are pursued for the Lord's glory, or for "Christ and His church" [p. 34].)*

3. Why can't Simon become a knight? *(Simon's father is a knight, which is an expensive occupation. Since he returned from battle injured and without his horse, the family has no money or land. Choosing a trade such as farming or blacksmithing would place Simon in a much lower social status, but he can retain his social position as a nobleman if he becomes a monk.)*

4. During the Crusades, Christians championed their faith in Christ through their actions, which they believed were noble based on the church's teachings. However, by fighting people of other faiths, the Crusaders were also passing judgment on those they considered "heathens." Discuss whether or not it is possible for people to defend their faith without condemning others' beliefs. *(Answers will vary. Some students may believe that tolerance of other people's values is certainly possible. Other students may strongly believe they should defend their own faith.)*

Supplementary Activities

1. History: Research the reign of King Richard I, or Richard the Lionheart. Complete an essay that details when he ruled, how he was perceived, and for what he is most famous. Also include any other significant details, such as how he received his nickname.

2. Art: Knights often carried shields into battle. Shields would traditionally display a symbol with a significant meaning. Research shields of the 1200s. Recreate the symbols of at least three shields, and describe the meaning of each one.

Edgar: The Falconer's Son

Edgar learns that the last sparrowhawk will be given to Simon, who is leaving the manor to become a monk. Edgar is dismayed that the bird he raised will soon be in Simon's care, for he doubts Simon's ability to care for the bird. Rather than give up the bird, Edgar chooses to free it, essentially stealing it from the lord, and he accepts the probable punishment for his action.

Vocabulary

jesses
qualm
mews
valor

Discussion Questions

1. What decision has Edgar made regarding the sparrowhawk? Why has he made this choice? Do you think this is wise? Why or why not? *(Edgar chooses to free the bird rather than place it in Simon's care. This equates to stealing the bird. He chooses to do this because he found and raised the bird and does not believe Simon will care for it. He believes that by "law of justice" the bird belongs to him, even though, in a true legal sense, it is the property of the master of the manor. Answers will vary.)*

2. Why has the master's manor gone bankrupt? *(In Simon's story, readers learn that the master, who is a knight, returned from battle with no horse and no money.)*

3. What have you learned about the role of a falconer on a manor? Is falconry (or hawking) a sport you might enjoy? Explain. *(Answers will vary. From the poem, students should have learned a little about the process of taming a bird and also about the falconer's importance to the manor. Falconers also enjoyed a higher social status than others on the manor because of the popularity of the sport of falconry.)*

Supplementary Activity

Music: Write a song of gratitude the sparrowhawk might sing to Edgar.

Isobel: The Lord's Daughter

Isobel finds herself in a dilemma—she cannot remove a stain from her gown, and she does not know who caused the stain by throwing dung at her. Rather than allow many to be punished for the offense, she tries to hide the evidence. She is unsettled by the hatred she feels from the peasants and tries to justify her status to herself.

Vocabulary

clod
sniggering
selfsame
churls

Discussion Questions

1. What do you make of Isobel's character? What does she value? Is she compassionate and kind or overly proud, or a combination of both? Explain. *(Answers will vary. The text indicates that Isobel values justice. She does not want boys innocent of staining her gown to be punished. She believes that she is justified in being better dressed and fed than others because it is the will of God. She displays acts of kindness to the poor, as she has been taught to do. She believes about her role what she has been told and tries to live her life accordingly. Some students, however, may feel her tone is unconsciously elitist.)*

2. Why do you think Isobel says, "The Lord God/chose my father to rule/the same way he chose them to serve" (p. 43)? Do you agree or disagree with her belief? *(Isobel believes what she has been taught—that people are placed into a specific social status according to God's will. Some students may argue that God would not "favor" some people over others. This argument is based on the individual's belief in the nature of God. Other students may argue that God can affect circumstances because he is omnipotent. Still others may disagree because they do not believe in God. Encourage students to give reasons for their opinions. Also, maintain an open discussion that does not lend itself to students belittling or attempting to alter others' beliefs. Students who do not wish to share information about their personal faith should not be pressured to do so.)*

3. Isobel feels hatred from others in the town because of her privileged status. Imagine you are a peasant on the manor. Knowing very little about Isobel and understanding your own circumstances, what would you think of the master's daughter? Would you be one of the children throwing things at her or not? Do you believe privileged people are persecuted today because of the advantages they have? Explain. *(Answers will vary.)*

Supplementary Activity

Art: Research the types of clothes people wore in the Middle Ages. Paint or sketch the dress Isobel might have worn in town. Also, create a picture of the type of clothes the peasant boys who laughed at Isobel might have worn.

Barbary: The Mud Slinger

Barbary expresses remorse over slinging mud at the lord's daughter. She also explains her own circumstances—she must buy fish and care for her younger twin siblings. In highlighting the differences between herself and Isobel, Barbary also notes the trials all women of the Middle Ages had to endure.

Vocabulary
folly
midden
staunch
smutch

Discussion Questions

1. Based on this story, discuss how giving birth during the Middle Ages was similar and different than it is now. *(Answers may vary. The risk of death in childbirth was much higher then than now. Also, Barbary's reference to "the pain" indicates that there were no painkillers available for childbirth. However, the stress of raising a family seems common to all ages. Students may also note from the last line that people then did not know the sex of a baby or even if they were having twins until the day of the delivery.)*

2. What do you learn of Barbary's character in this poem? If you were Barbary, would you have made the effort to apologize to Isobel? *(Answers will vary. Barbary is a tired, frustrated young girl who is perhaps envious of Isobel's easy life, especially compared to her own. Her mudslinging is vengeful, though she feels remorseful immediately. Readers see in Barbary the ability to be both sly and decent. Students should be aware of the beating Barbary could suffer if she confesses her crime and finds Isobel unforgiving.)*

3. What figurative language does the author use in this poem? Identify some examples, and discuss how they are useful in the poem. *(The poem includes many similes, such as "wailed like a babe" [p. 46], "sleek as an otter" [p. 47], "lips were curved,/like the smile of a cat" [p. 47], and "her back was straight as a knife" [p. 48]. The first simile also employs irony, as Barbary's mother is crying because she will be having another baby. The last three similes are meant to convey Isobel's nobility, and perhaps snobbery, from Barbary's point of view.)*

4. When praying for forgiveness for throwing the "muck" at the lord's daughter, why does Barbary also pray that her stepmother does not die? *(Answers will vary. Suggestions—This refers to the footnote at the beginning of the poem about the danger of childbirth. It also indicates Barbary may be afraid her action will cause the death of someone in her family. Finally, she might realize that she will have to raise her siblings if her stepmother dies.)*

5. How did you feel about Isobel's ruined dress after reading Isobel's account of the incident? How do you feel after reading Barbary's account? Discuss whether your feelings remained the same after reading Barbary's account and why. *(Answers will vary. Some may feel sympathetic toward Isobel after reading her account of the situation. After reading Barbary's story and realizing young boys did not haphazardly sling mud at Isobel, readers may have more compassion for the perpetrator as well as the victim. Encourage students to note the subtle lesson of the two poems: Consider both sides of a situation before making a judgment.)*

6. What type of conflict do both Barbary and Isobel experience as a result of the mudslinging incident? Explain how the conflicts are similar. *(Answers will vary. Both Barbary and Isobel experience a person vs. self conflict—Barbary because she was rude to Isobel, and Isobel because she is hated and wonders how to deal with the mudslinger.)*

Supplementary Activities
1. Writing: Identify a significant emotion Barbary experiences when seeing Isobel. Write a poem describing this emotion.
2. Research: Find information about medieval markets and modern events such as the Medieval Market of Turku, and then create a poster to advertise a market. Include handicrafts, performances, and exhibitions that will be featured at your market, as well as art or photographs of the medieval fashions worn by both knights and peasants.

Jacob ben Salomon: The Moneylender's Son and Petronella: The Merchant's Daughter

Jacob, a Jew, sees Petronella, a Christian, on the other side of a stream. Rather than intimidating one another, they enjoy each other's company until church bells summon Petronella away. Both have previously experienced or participated in acts of prejudice because Christians and Jews did not trust one another, so both vow to remain silent about their surprisingly pleasant meeting.

Discussion Questions
1. In form, how is this chapter different from the others? Discuss why it is structured as it is and how it is meant to be read. *(This chapter is not a monologue but a dialogue intended for two people. Readers read from left to right. Where one column is empty, that person is silent. Where there are words for both characters on the same line, readers read the words in unison. This may require practice for presentation.)*

Vocabulary
shoal
guild
convert

2. What unspoken conflict exists between Jacob and Petronella? How do they know this conflict exists when neither actually speaks of it? *(Their conflict is that each is of a different religion—Jacob is a Jew, and Petronella is a Christian. Petronella knows that Jacob is a Jew because he must wear a yellow patch on his clothes as identification. Additionally, both children have learned that Jews and Christians are not supposed to interact. Jacob has learned this by being persecuted by Christians, and Petronella has learned this because she has seen other Christians persecute Jews and has even thrown rocks at Jews herself.)*

3. How do the two children interact? What effect does their encounter have? *(They end up playing together, skipping rocks across the stream and laughing. Petronella begins to see Jacob as someone she could befriend. Jacob sees Petronella as more sympathetic than he would have thought, knowing she is Christian. Their friendly interaction helps them see beyond the historical tension between their religions.)*

4. Why did Jewish moneylenders charge high interest rates to their borrowers? *(Because Christians did not always pay back their Jewish lenders, a Jewish person could completely lose the money he lent to a Christian. Thus Jewish lenders tried to make as much money as possible on loans, particularly since they could not own land or participate in the guild system.)*

Supplementary Activity

1. Writing: Write a poem explaining how it probably felt to belong to a religious minority during the Middle Ages or what it would be like today. Read and compare different poems written by students in your class. Identify similarities and differences between poems written about the past and the present.

Lowdy: The Varlet's Child

Lowdy, who is the daughter of the man who tends the lord's hounds, talks about her life, her love of puppies, and her ongoing battle with fleas.

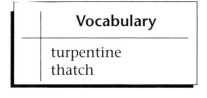

Discussion Questions

1. What is Lowdy's main problem? How has Lowdy tried to solve this problem? *(Fleas infest her home due to her family's close association with the master's dogs—it is a person vs. nature conflict. Lowdy has tried many remedies, cleaning solutions, and even prayer to get rid of the fleas, all to no avail.)*

2. What do you learn about housekeeping during medieval times from Lowdy's story? *(Lowdy's story shows that basic hygiene was difficult to maintain during medieval times. Keeping a clean house not only meant dusting and scrubbing but also removing unwanted creatures from one's living space. Homes could be bug-infested during the Middle Ages because people did not exterminate for fleas, maggots, lice, and other pests.)*

Supplementary Activity

History: Research the role of hounds in a medieval manor. Why was it important for lords to raise hounds? Write an essay reporting your findings.

Pask: The Runaway

Pask runs away from his overbearing lord after both of his parents die. He suffers through the winter but finds a friend in the varlet's daughter, Lowdy. He is determined to achieve independence and return to Lowdy a free man.

Vocabulary
dregs
vagabond
temperament

Discussion Questions

1. What obstacles must Pask face to become free? *(He must live in town for a year and a day. This means he must survive all four seasons, including the bitterly cold winter. Because he cannot work and must stay out of sight of his lord, who might be pursuing him, he has no money and no land to work. Additionally, Pask's parents have passed away, which means he has no family to help him survive. He often finds himself very hungry.)*

2. Why does Pask choose to run away while he is still a child? *(Pask's father once told him that it is easier to run away when you have only yourself to care for and that once a person has a family, he will do anything to care for them, even if it means working for an unfair lord.)*

3. Who gives Pask food in the kennels during the winter? How do you know? *(Lowdy; Pask describes her as a girl who works in the kennels. As the daughter of the varlet, Lowdy would work in the kennels. Also, he mentions that she loves the puppies, which Lowdy also mentions in her own story.)*

4. Do you think Pask will be able to make a living in town once he is a free man? Why or why not? *(Answers will vary. The background information informs readers that to learn a trade, many craftsmen required their apprentices to pay them. Pask has no money to pay with, but this does not mean he won't succeed in town.)*

Supplementary Activities

1. History: Research the calendar of celebrations during the Middle Ages. Identify when Eastertide, Lammas, Michaelmas, Lent, and Christmas were. Create a visual aid such as a time line to help you understand the beginning of Pask's story.

2. Health: One food that Pask mentions is a meat pie. Find the recipe for a medieval meat pie. With the help of an adult, make this dish for your classmates to taste.

Piers: The Glassblower's Apprentice

Piers is eager to blow glass on his own. When the wise glassblower finally allows him the chance to do so, Piers finds the task much more difficult than he anticipated. He is humbled.

Vocabulary
stoking
peevish
slothful

Discussion Questions

1. How does the author create a sense of tension in the monologue? *(The author portrays the art of glassblowing as dangerous by describing the glassblower's one eye. The description of Piers' first attempt at glassblowing is told piece by piece, leaving readers wondering if he will succeed, fail, or become harmed in the process of working with dangerously hot metal and glass.)*

2. Why does the apprentice pray that his master stays well? *(Piers is humbled by his first attempt at blowing glass. He realizes it truly is much harder than it looks and knows he is not yet ready to take on the role of glassblower alone. He needs the master to stay well in order to teach him.)*
3. Which other character(s) in the book do you think Piers might befriend? Why? *(Answers will vary. Students should look for characters with similarities to Piers, such as other orphans like Pask, other apprentices like Thomas, or others who have similar social statuses or goals like Edgar. Encourage students to give reasons for their opinions.)*

Supplementary Activities
1. Art: Find pictures of handblown glass art such as vases, lamps, bowls, and ornaments. Make a collage showing your findings.
2. Research: Explore the process of glassblowing online. Briefly summarize the process by including some key terms associated with the art, such as molten, furnace, and parison.

Mariot and Maud: The Glassblower's Daughters

Both daughters are aware that for Piers to inherit their father's business, Piers must marry one of them. Maud, the younger daughter, cannot imagine marrying Piers and believes her sister feels the same way. However, through the dialogue, readers discover that Mariot would be very willing to marry Piers.

Vocabulary
awry
tunic
churlish

Discussion Questions
1. Mariot seems kinder toward Piers from the beginning than her sister Maud does. How do you account for their difference of opinion? *(Answers will vary. Maud states outright that she does not like Piers. However, she is also the younger of the two sisters. She may not be at an age where marriage or boys are of interest to her yet. Mariot is older and understands why Piers behaves the way he does—she mentions that he is an orphan, and she does not interpret his silence as rudeness, as Maud does. Mariot also seems to value highly her father's opinions of people.)*
2. How does the author incorporate humor into the dialogue? *(Answers will vary. The author overlaps each sister's statements so that it seems one sister is finishing the other's thought when, in reality, each is unaware of the other's speech. For example, Mariot begins a statement that she should "treat [Piers] with" and Maud states, "earwax," while Mariot's own ending to her sentence is "courtesy" [pp. 71–72].)*
3. Discuss arranged marriages in which a person marries based on social position or to preserve a family business. *(Discussions will vary. Note that arranged marriages are still common in some cultures today.)*

Supplementary Activity
History: Most people in medieval times were very poor. Research traditions of a common medieval marriage ceremony. What typically occurred during the ceremony? Was there a celebration afterwards, and if so, what was it like? Also, research what people wore to a wedding. After sharing your findings with classmates, compare and contrast marriage ceremonies of the Middle Ages with those today.

Nelly: The Sniggler

Nelly tells the story of how she survived as a baby and brought her family good luck. She describes her family's business collecting eels and also her ongoing frustrations with Drogo, the tanner's apprentice.

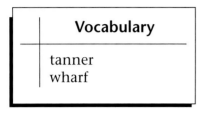

Vocabulary

tanner
wharf

Discussion Questions

1. Nelly's parents felt the only thing to do with a baby they could not feed was drown it. Fortunately, Nelly miraculously survives. What options does our culture offer parents who deliver a baby but feel they cannot adequately care for the child? *(Answers will vary. In America, parents can put a baby up for adoption. Should they keep the child, parents can also register for government assistance that will help them receive food and medical care for the child.)*

2. What insight does Nelly give regarding a medieval diet? Discuss how Nelly's diet is similar to or different from your own. What is your opinion of medieval food? What do you think people like Nelly would think of your diet? *(Nelly speaks of eels and frogs as being highly-prized food sources. The author indicates that they were valued because of the protein they provided. Encourage students to think about their common sources of meat/protein such as beef, pork, beans, fish, and chicken, and encourage them to think about how Nelly or other characters would view our modern diet.)*

3. Do you think Nelly really dislikes Drogo as much as she says she does? Explain. *(Answers will vary. Some students may agree with Nelly's statements. Others may think she likes him but shows it by teasing and intentionally ignoring him.)*

Supplementary Activity

Character: Nelly almost dies because her parents are afraid they won't be able to care for her. Conduct research to find an organization that helps poverty-stricken families around the world. Report to the class about the work the organization does to help children and parents. The organization can provide medical care, clean water, food, educational support, AIDS relief, orphan care, and more. Together with your teacher, organize a charity drive publicizing the organization and the work it does, and send any funds raised to this organization.

Drogo: The Tanner's Apprentice

Drogo discusses the advantages and disadvantages of being a tanner.

Vocabulary
nattering
tallow

Discussion Questions

1. What is Drogo's attitude toward his work? Why does he feel as he does? *(Drogo does not mind his work, even if it is not clean or easy. He is proud to make things people need. He also appreciates the money he makes, which allows him to live well. However, he dislikes people who complain about the way tanning byproducts pollute rivers. Answers will vary.)*

2. Are the townspeople justified in complaining about pollution from tanning animal hides? How does Drogo view the way tanners treat the waters? *(Answers will vary. Drogo seems to indicate that, while his work does put chemicals into the water, it is necessary in order to produce things from hides. For him, the ends justify the means. He sees the hypocrisy in people who use the things he makes but complain about how he makes them.)*

Supplementary Activities

1. Debate: Some people today are against using animal hides to make things. Other people disagree. Choose a side. Conduct research to support your position. Form small groups, and engage in a class debate about the issue. The resolution for debate is: It is justified to use animal skins for human purposes. The affirmative side will agree with the resolution. The negative side will disagree with the resolution. Allow your teacher to set the format, determining how much time each side will have to present its case and to refute the opposition. Classmates listening to the debate will vote on the winner.

2. Environmental Science: The author notes that water pollution is not a new dilemma. Conduct research about a water source (river, lake, etc.) or natural habitat (nature park, etc.) in your area or just outside of your city. Find information about community cleanup projects for the area you select, and publicize the dates for your peers. If you cannot find a cleanup project near your area, work with your teacher to organize a school cleanup day in which you and your peers work to make your school property a cleaner, healthier environment.

Giles: The Beggar

Giles explains how he and his father deceive those they encounter to gain enough money to survive.

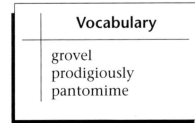

Discussion Questions

1. What is the purpose of parentheses in this poem? How might students read the parenthetical phrases differently from the rest of the story? *(The author uses parentheses to help readers depict the difference between Giles' reality and the show he and his father put on in hopes of earning money. Giles is giving insight into the trickery of their act. The "act" should be read with emotion to evoke sympathy from the audience, while the lines in parentheses may be spoken under one's breath or in a secretive, conspiratorial manner.)*

2. Is Giles' foot truly wounded? Explain in your own words how Giles and his father trick people into giving them money. *(Giles' foot is not truly injured, though he pretends it is in order to receive pity from others. When people ignore him, he pretends to collapse. His father then comes along, but no one in the town knows the two are related. His father begins trying to sell a remedy of holy water and some saintly artifacts to the people. To prove his remedy works, he uses it on his son's foot. His son pretends to be cured by the holy water. Giles then leaves town while the townspeople pay his father for drops of the holy water. Later, father and son reunite to share the pay from their act.)*

3. Why do Giles and his father pray that the Lord looks after the foxes as well as the sheep? *(This is a metaphorical analogy likening Giles and his father to foxes who prey upon sheep, or the gullible townspeople. They are asking God's protection even though they take advantage of the rest of the "flock.")*

Supplementary Activity

Drama: In pairs, reenact Giles' and his father's charade. Note the differences between performing a monologue and acting out a part. For example, you move more when you act, lines must be memorized, and there is no narrator.

Post-reading Discussion Questions

1. Was there a difference between reading the stories to yourself and seeing/hearing them performed? Explain. *(Answers will vary.)*

2. Discuss whether or not the book is effective in portraying a specific time in history. Use examples from the text to support your position. What history did you learn from reading the book? Are there additional questions you have about the Middle Ages or any other time period as a result of reading the book? *(Answers will vary. Students could have learned various historical details regarding trades of people in a medieval village, the caste system, and more.)*

3. Based on what you learned from the book, discuss the role that religion played in medieval life. Give examples from the characters' stories. *(Answers will vary. Note that the Catholic tradition was very strong in medieval times. Religious beliefs dictated many decisions people made; for example, Constance makes a pilgrimage to a well to find healing. Religion also influenced actions: Thomas' father prays for his patients, and Jacob and Petronella keep their meeting a secret because of their different religions. A person's standing with God was an ever-present concern [Barbary prays for forgiveness, Isobel justifies her social status, and Giles' father hopes for favor despite his deceit.].)*

4. Of all the occupations you read about, which sounds most appealing to you, and why? *(Answers will vary. Encourage students to consider actual occupations and not just choose to be "nobility.")*

5. Of the 23 characters in the book, how many experience a death in the family? How does this loss affect the characters' lives? *(Answers will vary. Some deaths are mentioned, while others can be assumed. Will must take his father's place in the field; Mogg and Jack must survive without their father, who is not missed due to his violence; Otho's grandfather was murdered, and Otho will follow his grandfather's trade as a miller; Simon's father is injured in battle, and Simon is forced to become a monk instead of a knight; Barbary is without a mother and must help her stepmother raise her siblings; Pask is an orphan in hiding; Piers is an orphaned assistant studying glassblowing. The loss of life obviously made more work for youngsters, as Will laments in his statement: "I don't know why the fields have the right to rest when people don't" [p. 10]. The death of a parent or relative results in poverty, bitterness, and desperation for most, but there are also moments of goodness and cleverness, as when Mogg's family saves their cow.)*

6. Discuss which natural resources were critical to people's survival during the Middle Ages. Are those same resources critical today? *(Water was important, as there is much discussion about the tanner's pollution of the river water. Healthy soil was important for growing crops, which is why plowmen rotated crops. Additionally, sources of protein were very valuable, such as eels and frogs. Communities/manors needed to be as self-sufficient as possible because travelling far away to trade was difficult. Answers will vary, although most students will probably agree that these natural resources, along with others such as fossil fuels, timber, and metals, are still vital today.)*

7. Discuss the similarities and differences between your life and that of village youngsters. *(Answers will vary. Encourage students to give examples when appropriate. Suggestions—The book highlights youngsters of the village who recognize their commonalities, despite their differences. For example, Jacob and Petronella end up getting along despite religious differences, boys of slightly different social ranking become secret friends as they bond due to abuse they suffer from their fathers, and Barbary realizes all women—peasants and noblewomen—must face the dangers of childbirth. Similarly, people today can relate to one another, despite their differences. Just as in 1255, today there are poor people and wealthy people. There are children with kind parents and children with abusive parents. People then and now live with blended families, though the reason for having a blended family may be different.)*

8. Do you think the overlapping of some characters' stories added or detracted from the book? Explain. *(Answers will vary. Some students may think the stories of Isobel and Barbary, for example, provided an interesting contrast of perspective on the same situation and between the lives of young nobles and peasants.)*

9. Discuss the author's use of footnotes in the book. Were they helpful? Did they add or detract from the book? Discuss the value of footnotes in historical fiction. *(Answers will vary. Point out the historical notes in the margins as well as the brief essays on topics such as falconry and the Crusades. Students will probably notice that the footnotes and essays give background and context, sometimes humorously.)*

10. Discuss why you think this book won the Newbery Medal. Identify some qualities of excellent young adult literature. Does this book meet those requirements? What would you want to include in a book that would qualify as "excellent" young adult literature? *(Answers will vary. Newbery Award criteria include: The book must display respect for children's understandings, abilities, and appreciations, be individually unique and marked by excellence, be appropriate in style, and more.)*

11. What is the main theme or message you think the author communicates to readers of this book? *(Answers will vary. Suggestions—Some may believe the author gives students insight into another time. Others may think she gives insight into the human condition by showing that people across the ages have similar life experiences.)*

12. Describe the style of illustrator Robert Byrd in this book. What purpose does the historical detail in the art serve? What other books has Byrd illustrated? *(Answers will vary. The inside cover states that Byrd based his work on a thirteenth-century German manuscript. Point out the patterned boarders, the square miniatures, and the ink and watercolor illustrations that resemble woodcuts. Although Byrd's style hints at the medieval period, the realistic scenes are contemporary. Other books Byrd has illustrated include* Leonardo, Beautiful Dreamer; Finn MacCoul and His Fearless Wife, The Hero and the Minotaur, *and many more.)*

Post-reading Extension Activities

Research
1. Research a medieval holiday celebration. Use visual aids to explain the holiday and how people celebrated it. If it is a holiday we still celebrate today, highlight similarities and differences between how it is celebrated now and how it was celebrated then.
2. The nobleman's son wanted to be a knight but was instead forced to be a monk to preserve his social status. Conduct research to compare and contrast the lives of monks and knights during medieval times. Present your findings in a Venn diagram.
3. Create five original footnotes for the book that would increase a reader's understanding of the characters' lives. Use various sources to research your facts about feudalism, markets, diseases, or other aspects of medieval culture.

Music
4. Research music in medieval times. Report on popular medieval instruments or songs. If possible, bring an example of music medieval people would have heard or sung.

Writing
5. Learn about a trade in medieval times other than one mentioned in the book. Write your own monologue for a medieval youngster who works in that trade.
6. Choose two characters from the book who have not met, and write a short story about them. How will the characters meet? What will they say? How will they treat one another, and why?

Cooking
7. Research a medieval recipe. Prepare the dish for your class to sample. (Note: Students should have adult assistance when preparing the dish. Teachers should be aware of student allergies before permitting the class to sample the food.)

Art
8. Paint a vivid picture of a scene from one of the stories in the book.
9. Create a diorama depicting one of the scenes in the book.
10. Select a character. Write down ideas for several props appropriate to that character's story. Draw or design a suitable costume that is true to the time period and the social status of the character.

Assessment for *Good Masters! Sweet Ladies!*

Assessment is an ongoing process. The following nine items can be completed during study of the novel. Once finished, the student and teacher will check the work. Points may be added to indicate the level of understanding.

Name _____ Date _____

Student   **Teacher**

_____   _____   1. Complete an Attribute Web as you brainstorm about the feudal system of medieval England. What were the social tiers? Who fit into the different tiers? See page 32 of this guide.

_____   _____   2. Complete the Thematic Analysis web for the book. See page 33 of this guide.

_____   _____   3. Complete the Conflict chart using as many different characters as you can. See page 34 of this guide.

_____   _____   4. Complete the Character Web for one of the characters in the book. You may even use this information to help you prepare for performing your monologue or dialogue. See page 35 of this guide.

_____   _____   5. Write a review of the book using at least five vocabulary words from this guide.

_____   _____   6. Identify two values that multiple characters in the book possess. Give reasons for why you chose these values, identify which characters possess them, and give evidence from the book supporting your opinion.

_____   _____   7. Choose an event that happens to one or more of the characters in the book. Write a newspaper article detailing what happened, to whom, and why the event is significant or newsworthy for the rest of the manor.

_____   _____   8. List at least ten characters from the book. Identify how each fits into life on the manor, and tell a small portion of each one's story.

_____   _____   9. Complete any tests or quizzes taken over the book.

Pros and Cons

Directions: Use the chart below to brainstorm the pros and cons of living during the Middle Ages.

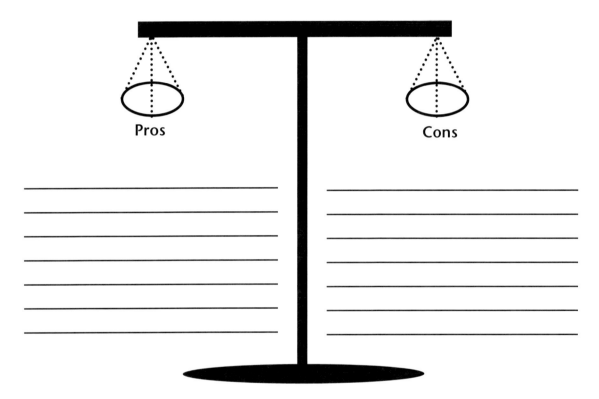

Attribute Web

Directions: Complete the attribute web by filling in your ideas about the feudal system during the Middle Ages.

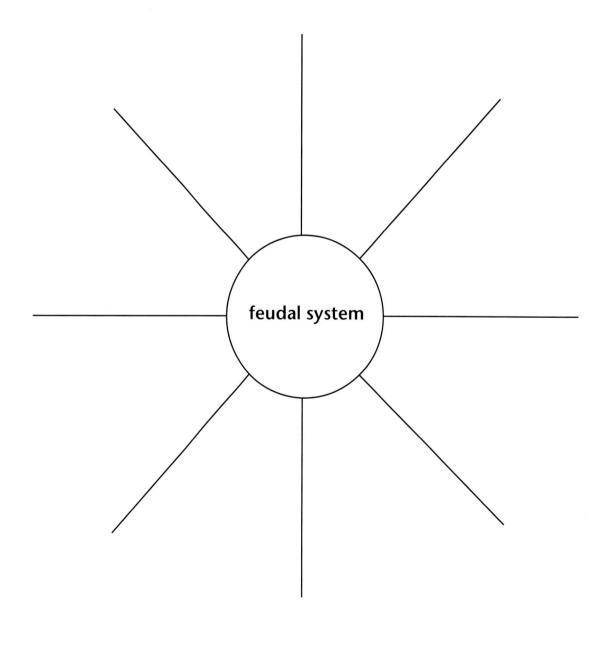

Thematic Analysis

Directions: Choose a theme from the book to be the focus of your word web. Complete the web and then answer the question in each starred box.

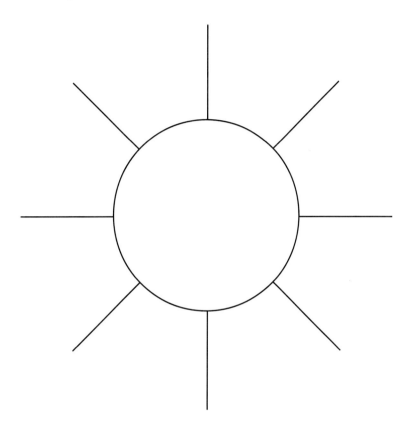

 What is the author's main message?

 What did you learn from the book?

Conflict

The **conflict** of a story is the struggle between two people or two forces. There are four main types of conflict: person vs. person, person vs. nature, person vs. society, and person vs. self.

Directions: In the space provided, list four conflicts a character experiences and justify why you identify it with that particular type of conflict. Then explain how each conflict is resolved in the story.

person vs. person

Conflict	Resolution

person vs. nature

Conflict	Resolution

person vs. society

Conflict	Resolution

person vs. self

Conflict	Resolution

Character Web

Directions: Choose a character from the novel and complete the chart below. Cite evidence from the story as you fill in information. If the book does not provide enough evidence to complete the chart, use your imagination to develop your character. You may even use the chart to help you understand the character you will portray when you perform the character's monologue/dialogue for the class.

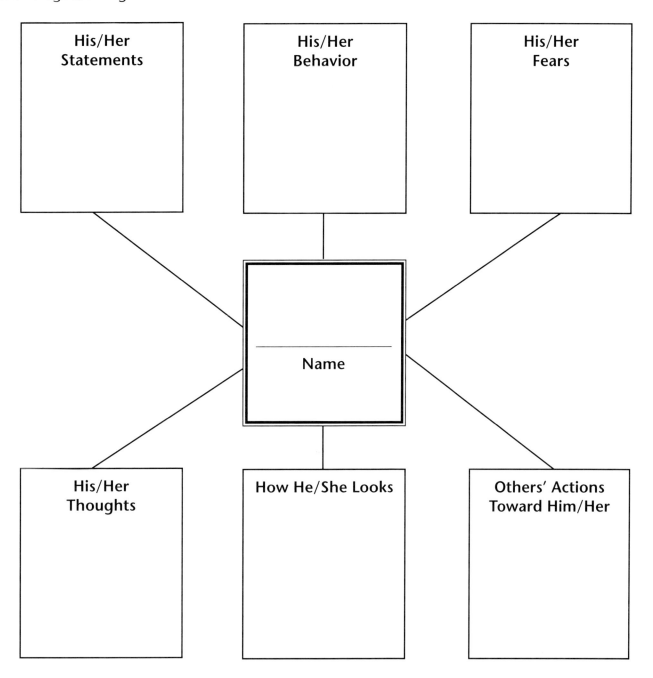

Linking Novel Units® Lessons to National and State Reading Assessments

During the past several years, an increasing number of students have faced some form of state-mandated competency testing in reading. Many states now administer state-developed assessments to measure the skills and knowledge emphasized in their particular reading curriculum. The discussion questions and post-reading questions in this Novel Units® Teacher Guide make excellent open-ended comprehension questions and may be used throughout the daily lessons as practice activities. The rubric below provides important information for evaluating responses to open-ended comprehension questions. Teachers may also use scoring rubrics provided for their own state's competency test.

Please note: The Novel Units® Student Packet contains optional open-ended questions in a format similar to many national and state reading assessments.

Scoring Rubric for Open-Ended Items

3-Exemplary
- Thorough, complete ideas/information
- Clear organization throughout
- Logical reasoning/conclusions
- Thorough understanding of reading task
- Accurate, complete response

2-Sufficient
- Many relevant ideas/pieces of information
- Clear organization throughout most of response
- Minor problems in logical reasoning/conclusions
- General understanding of reading task
- Generally accurate and complete response

1-Partially Sufficient
- Minimally relevant ideas/information
- Obvious gaps in organization
- Obvious problems in logical reasoning/conclusions
- Minimal understanding of reading task
- Inaccuracies/incomplete response

0-Insufficient
- Irrelevant ideas/information
- No coherent organization
- Major problems in logical reasoning/conclusions
- Little or no understanding of reading task
- Generally inaccurate/incomplete response